Cancer

Also by Sally Kirkman

Aries
Taurus
Gemini
Leo
Virgo
Libra
Scorpio
Sagittarius
Capricorn
Aquarius
Pisces

SALLY KIRKMAN

Cancer

The Art of Living Well and Finding
Happiness According to Your Star Sign

HODDER

First published in Great Britain in 2018 by Hodder & Stoughton
An Hachette UK company

1

Copyright © Sally Kirkman 2018

The right of Sally Kirkman to be identified as the Author of the
Work has been asserted by her in accordance with the Copyright,
Designs and Patents Act 1988.

All images © Shutterstock.com

A CIP catalogue record for this title is available from the British Library

Hardback ISBN 978 1 473 67673 2

Typeset in Celeste 11.5/17 pt by Palimpsest Book Production Limited,
Falkirk, Stirlingshire

Printed in the United States of America by LSC Communications

Hodder & Stoughton policy is to use papers that are natural,
renewable and recyclable products and made from wood grown in
sustainable forests. The logging and manufacturing processes are expected
to conform to the environmental regulations of the country of origin.

Hodder & Stoughton Ltd
Carmelite House
50 Victoria Embankment
London EC4Y 0DZ

www.hodder.co.uk

Contents

• • • • •

Introduction

• • • • •

Before computers, books or a shared language, people were fascinated by the movement of the stars and planets. They created stories and myths around them. We know that the Babylonians were one of the first people to record the zodiac, a few hundred years BC.

In ancient times, people experienced a close connection to the earth and the celestial realm. The adage 'As above, so below', that the movement of the planets and stars mirrored life on earth and human affairs, made perfect sense. Essentially, we were all one, and ancient people sought symbolic meaning in everything around them.

We are living in a very different world now, in

which scientific truth is paramount; yet many people are still seeking meaning. In a world where you have an abundance of choice, dominated by the social media culture that allows complete visibility into other people's lives, it can be hard to feel you belong or find purpose or think that the choices you are making are the right ones.

It's this calling for something more, the sense that there's a more profound truth beyond the objective and scientific, that leads people to astrology and similar disciplines that embrace a universal truth, an intuitive knowingness. Today astrology has a lot in common with spirituality, meditation, the Law of Attraction, a desire to know the cosmic order of things.

Astrology means 'language of the stars' and people today are rediscovering the usefulness of ancient wisdom. The universe is always talking to you; there are signs if you listen and the more you tune in, the more you feel guided by life. This is one of astrology's significant benefits, helping you to make sense of an increasingly unpredictable world.

Used well, astrology can guide you in making the best possible decisions in your life. It's an essential skill in your personal toolbox that enables you to navigate the ups and downs of life consciously and efficiently.

About this book

Astrology is an ancient art that helps you find meaning in the world. The majority of people to this day know their star sign, and horoscopes are growing increasingly popular in the media and online.

The modern reader understands that star signs are a helpful reference point in life. They not only offer valuable self-insight and guidance, but are indispensable when it comes to understanding other people, and living and working together in harmony.

This new and innovative pocket guide updates the ancient tradition of astrology to make it relevant and topical for today. It distils the wisdom of the star signs into an up-to-date format that's easy to read and digest, and fun and informative too. Covering a broad range of topics, it offers you insight and understanding into many different areas of your life. There are some unique sections you won't find anywhere else.

The style of the guide is geared towards you being able to maximise your strengths, so you can live well and use your knowledge of your star sign to your advantage. The more in tune you are with your zodiac sign, the higher your potential to lead a happy and fulfilled life.

The guide starts with a quick introduction to your star sign, in bullet point format. This not only reveals your star sign's ancient ruling principles, but brings astrology up-to-date, with your star sign mission, an appropriate quote for your sign and how best to describe your star sign in a tweet.

The first chapter is called 'Be True To Your Sign' and is one of the most important sections in the guide. It's a comprehensive look at all aspects of your star sign, helping define what makes you special, and explaining how the rich symbolism of your zodiac sign can reveal more about your character. For example, being born at a specific time of year and in a particular season is significant in itself.

This chapter focuses in depth on the individual attributes of your star sign in a way that's positive and uplifting. It offers a holistic view of your sign and is meant to inspire you. Within this section, you find out the reasons why your star sign traits and characteristics are unique to you.

There's a separate chapter towards the end of the guide that takes this star sign information to a new level. It's called 'Your Cosmic Gifts and Talents' and tells you what's individual about you from your star sign perspective. Most importantly, it highlights your skills and strengths, offering you clear examples of how to make the most of your natural birthright.

The guide touches on another important aspect of your star sign, in the chapters entitled 'Your Shadow Side' and 'Your Star Sign Secrets'. This reveals the potential weaknesses inherent within your star sign, and the tricks and habits you can fall into if you're not aware of them. The star sign secrets might surprise you.

There's guidance here about what you can focus on to minimise the shadow side of your star sign, and this is linked in particular to your opposite sign of the zodiac. You learn how opposing forces complement each other when you hold both ends of the spectrum, enabling them to work together.

Essentially, the art of astrology is about how to find balance in your life, to gain a sense of universal or cosmic order, so you feel in flow rather than pulled in different directions.

Other chapters in the guide provide revealing information about your love life and sex life. There are cosmic tips on how to work to your star sign strengths so you can attract and keep a fulfilling relationship, and lead a joyful sex life. There's also a guide to your love compatibility with all twelve star signs.

Career, money and prosperity is another essential section in the guide. These chapters offer you vital information on your purpose in life, and how to make the most of your potential out in the world. Your star sign skills and strengths are revealed, including what sort of job or profession suits you.

There are also helpful suggestions about what to avoid and what's not a good choice for you. There's a list of traditional careers associated with your star sign, to give you ideas about where you can excel in life if you require guidance on your future direction.

Also, there are chapters in the book on practical matters, like your health and well-being, your food and diet. These recommend the right kind of exercise for you, and how you can increase your vitality and nurture your mind, body and soul, depending on your star sign. There are individual yoga poses and tarot cards that have been carefully selected for you.

Further chapters reveal unique star sign information about your image and style. This includes whether there's a particular fashion that suits you, and how you can accentuate your look and make the most of your body.

There are even chapters that can help you decide where to go on holiday and who with, and how to decorate your home. There are some fun sections, including ideal gifts for your star sign, and ideas for films, books and music specific to your star sign.

Also, the guide has a comprehensive birthday section so you can find out which famous people share your birthday. You can discover who else is born under your star sign, people who may be your role models and whose careers or gifts you can aspire to. There are celebrity examples throughout the guide too, revealing more about the unique characteristics of your star sign.

At the end of the guide, there's a Question and Answer section, which explains the astrological terms used in the guide. It also offers answers to some general questions that often arise around astrology.

This theme is continued in a useful section entitled Additional Information. This describes the symmetry of astrology and shows you how different patterns connect the twelve star signs. If you're a beginner to astrology, this is your next stage, learning about the elements, the modes and the houses.

View this book as your blueprint, your guide to you and your future destiny. Enjoy discovering astrological revelations about you, and use this pocket guide to learn how to live well and find happiness according to your star sign.

A QUICK GUIDE TO CANCER

• • • • •

Cancer Birthdays: 21 June to 22 July

Zodiac Symbol: The Crab

Ruling Planet: Moon

Mode/Element: Cardinal Water

Colour: Silver, white

Part of the Body: Breasts, chest and stomach

Day of the Week: Monday

Top Traits: Emotional, Reflective, Home-loving

Your Star Sign Mission: to nurture people and things into life; to care unconditionally

Best At: building 'family' connections at home and work, bonding, gathering the clans, making things grow, caring for people and animals, emotional artistry, reminiscing, archiving the past

Weaknesses: hoarding, clingy behaviour, snippy, a tendency to whinge, getting stuck in your comfort zone

Key Phrase: I care

Cancer Quote: 'And as we let our own light shine, we unconsciously give other people permission to do the same.' Nelson Mandela

How to describe Cancer in a Tweet: Sensitive, moody, waxes & wanes like the Moon. Loves comforting food & cosy nights in. Mummy's boy, Daddy's girl; family rules

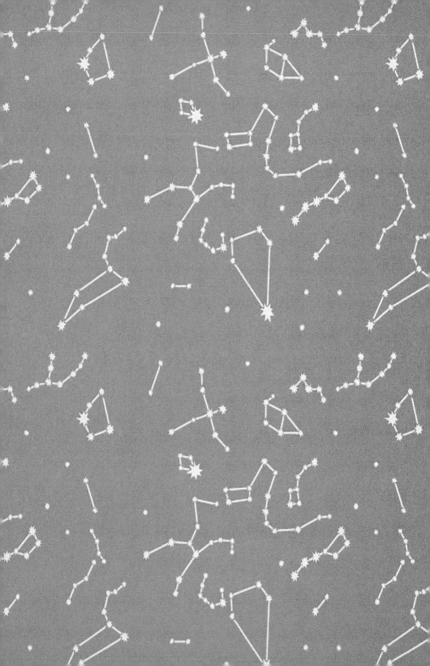

Be True To Your Sign

• • • • •

The Cancer individual is made up of a surging wave of emotion. Sensitive and caring, Cancer is the cuddliest of all the star signs and home and family almost always play a significant role in your life. You are in turn protective and cautious, reflective and giving, and your past and future are closely linked.

You are the only star sign of the zodiac to be ruled by the Moon, Queen of the night. The feminine Moon is the counterpart to the masculine Sun, and whereas the Sun rules the light of the day, the Moon rules the dark of the night. They are equally important.

The Moon's realm in astrology is shadowy and

witchy, representing the divine feminine; instincts and feelings are honoured above logic and thought. The Moon represents the subconscious and the dream world and is the yin to the Sun's yang, and the typical Cancer is a private individual, with a profound and complex inner life.

In some ancient cultures, the Moon was revered over the Sun, and many lunar (Moon) deities were worshipped. The astrological qualities associated with the Moon are kind, caring, protective, feminine energies, nurturing the people and the earth. These are excellent qualities for leadership, although not always admired in our current climate.

Your sign of Cancer is one of the four cardinal signs of the zodiac, along with Aries, Libra and Capricorn. Therefore, you are one of life's leaders, although you lead in your own unique way. Your sign belongs to the element water, ruling the emotions and the softer, more gentle flow of life.

Like the other cardinal signs, Cancer marks a change of season. The Sun moving into Cancer heralds the Solstice, one of the midway points in the year. In the northern hemisphere, it represents the height of summer; in the southern hemisphere, it denotes the middle of winter.

Some of the Moon goddesses were huntresses, at home and active in the dark of the night. Even though the classic Cancer archetype is a soft, cuddly character, there's a dominant side to your nature, like all of the cardinal signs, and you are perfectly capable of being self-sufficient.

Think of your zodiac symbol, the Crab, which carries its home on its back and has the tendency to withdraw and hide when it encounters a scary situation. The crab has a tough outer shell but a soft underbelly, and the same can be said for the Cancer archetype. You might look tough on the outside and act defensively, but you're soft and vulnerable on the inside.

What drives you more than anything is your love of home and family, and this extends to your clan, your people, your territory. Cancer rules the fourth house in astrology, which is at the base of the horoscope wheel.

This connects you to your ancestry, your predecessors; the fourth house rules not only home and family, but also your past and where you come from. This part of the horoscope is known as 'the womb to the tomb'.

Letting go of your past doesn't come easily to you, and the symbolic rubber band that ties you to family or history can be so tight that it keeps you from moving forward.

You are at your most fiercely protective, however, when it comes to the people you love. This is primarily your immediate family although it can extend to your employees, your country – wherever your loyalties lie. It is your profound ability to care for and nurture others that defines the quintessential Cancer.

Even though you have a private side to your nature and you need a place you can retreat to in life, it's unusual for a typical Cancer to enjoy being completely alone. This corresponds to your ruler-ship by the Moon, because the Moon's light is a reflection of the light of the Sun. In the same way, you need other people around you to draw you out into the world and to reflect back who you are; although, like all of the water signs, you have to learn to put up invisible barriers between yourself and other people, as your essential nature is emotional.

You're sensitive to other people's feelings; you feel their pain and their happiness; and your own emotions have a powerful effect on others too. If you're not to spend all day weeping or experi-encing an overflow of emotion, you have to learn to pull back at times from feelings that are sad or overwhelm you. You are known for wallowing in emotions and the past.

Your sign of Cancer is the most changeable in the zodiac. Your emotions ebb and flow; you can be moody one minute and calm the next. This fits the shape-shifting symbolism of the Moon, so different from the continuous circle of the Sun. The Moon's phases are visible to the naked eye, and you can tell when it's a new moon or a full moon by its shape in the sky.

The Moon has a powerful influence on our lives and, in astrology, it is a universal symbol of the mother, children and fertility. As a Cancer, you're at your best in a mothering or nurturing role or when you are encouraging other people or plants or a personal project to grow.

Of all the planetary bodies, there are more myths and romance surrounding the Moon than any other. You 'promise the moon', you 'reach for the moon' and you say 'I love you to the moon and back'.

Inherent within the Cancer archetype is a romantic, imaginative soul that honours past connections and loves deeply. You pour your emotions into everything you do, and your retentive nature holds on to things that would otherwise be lost.

The Cancer crab clings on tenaciously, refusing to let go. Similarly, the challenge for your sign is in trusting instinctively when the time is right to move on, knowing that sometimes you must release the past to embrace the future.

Your Shadow Side

If you're a typical Cancer, your sensitive nature means that you are often nervous of upsetting other people, and you can be very touchy and easily wounded if you feel offended by someone else's behaviour.

You often go out of your way to try to be helpful to other people, and you like to be seen as someone who's kind and non-judgemental. Having a complicated emotional life means that you rarely act straightforwardly.

Like your zodiac symbol, the Crab, who scuttles sideways, you too can cause yourself agony by trying to second-guess other people or divert away from the real issue, especially when it's contentious.

The end result is that you rarely respond directly and, more often than not, you get caught up playing emotional games. This can become exhausting and overwhelming for you, and exasperate the other person or people concerned.

Plus, there is a side of your nature that's cool, like the Moon. Think of your counterpart, the Sun, which is all heat and fire and constancy, while your ruler the Moon represents changeability; you're more likely to blow hot and cold.

Add to this the fact that your nature is to hold on tight and you can find it hard to let go of emotions like resentment and guilt. This can lead to veiled insults and, at its most extreme, cruel behaviour.

There is another factor too that adds to the complexity of your unpredictable Cancer nature. You put other people before yourself because you want to appear kind and caring, yet in the process, you often neglect your own emotional needs. This then quickly flips to anger or feeling sorry for yourself. There's that swing in mood and temperament again.

As your emotional relationships can be so complex, your default position is to retreat. If this becomes a habit, then your need for safety and security means you find it increasingly difficult to move out of your comfort zone. Sometimes you use other people as an excuse not to live your own life; or you'd simply rather stay hidden and, to some extent, invisible, than take huge risks and live life on the edge.

If this becomes ingrained behaviour, there is a danger that you could end your days with a huge sense of regret. So take a leaf out of your opposite sign's book, as this is where you can learn something new about yourself.

Your opposite sign is Capricorn, an earth sign, symbolising respect, dignity and status. Capricorns have a backbone, and they gravitate naturally towards positions of rank and take an active role out in the world. Capricorn is less emotional than your sign of Cancer, and it's rare for a Capricorn to let fear or a need for comfort to hold them back in life.

One of Cancer's important lessons to learn is that feeling secure in life is ultimately an inside job, and external circumstances count for little. Once you understand that your happiness and security comes from within, then you can stop allowing your emotions to hold you back and use them instead to benefit yourself and other people.

Your Star Sign Secrets

Shhh, don't tell anyone but your greatest fear is that other people will find out that you have a martyr complex. Martyrs are traditionally selfless, sacrificial and kind but when your full Cancer capacity for caring flips into extreme behaviour, you drop yourself out time and again. You pretend it's because you're a compassionate person who will do anything for other people. Scratch the surface, however, and playing the martyr invariably means that you don't have to take responsibility for your life, and you can outwardly blame others instead. This is Cancer's star sign secret.

You have another secret too, which is a longing to be free of all responsibilities. If you're a typical Cancer, you set up your life so you have people to look after and possessions to manage. There's a side to your nature, however, that wants to break out of any shyness you feel and be footloose and fancy-free, able to roam the world in style and do exactly what you want.

Your Love Life

Knowing about your star sign is an absolute essential when it comes to love and relationships. Once you understand what drives you, nurtures you and keeps you happy in love, then you can be true to who you are rather than try to be someone you're not.

Plus, once you recognise your weak points when it comes to relationships (and everyone has them), you can learn to moderate them and focus instead on boosting your strengths to find happiness in love.

> **KEY CONCEPTS:** the shy femme fatale, comfort and security, lasting love, clinging on too tight, cuddles and spooning all day long

Cosmic Tip: The Cancer shell is tough to penetrate, and emotions don't work. It's a person's intellect or wit that cracks you open.

If you're a typical Cancer, you have a shy side to your nature that means you're not usually the person going wild in the nightclub trying to catch other people's attention. Your dating approach is often more subtle and it can take you a while to pluck up courage to talk to someone you're attracted to. The eyes have it with all the water signs, Cancer included, and you know how to give a look that says 'I'm interested'.

Dating for you often takes place close to home because you're a creature of routine. If there's a bar or club you go to every week, then this is where you're most likely to meet someone new. This means you don't have to make up your mind straight away if there's someone you like; you can take your time if you know you'll see them again.

If you're looking for a long-term relationship, it's a good idea to ask your family or your close group of friends for an introduction. It can be important for you to meet a partner who shares your interests or has the same group of friends. This is especially true if you're getting ready to settle down.

It is rare for a Sun Cancer to stay single throughout their lifetime and in fact, yours is one of the star signs that want to be in a relationship. There's a side of your character that loves having someone to look after and who will take care of you. Cancer men often look for someone to mother them, and Cancer women often find someone who's strong with big arms and a big heart.

The classic Cancer loves nothing more than cuddles and affection and lying in your partner's arms, feeling protected and safe.

When you've found the person you want to partner in life, in your eyes it's for keeps. If you dream of having your own family, your own home, you will choose the person you think is most suitable, and a partner with good prospects fits the bill.

When you're coupled up, this is when the silly, cutesy side of your nature can be expressed to the full. You love to have a partner you can be romantic with, even childishly so, and it's not unusual for you and your loved one to have pet names for each other.

You might even have a heap of cuddly animals from your childhood, but perhaps when you meet someone special, it's time to let them go. For the classic Cancer, a loving relationship can be a welcome escape from the outside world where you have to play the adult.

Your essential nature is sentimental, and you are usually traditional when it comes to relationships. You want to do things the 'right' way, including a regular courtship, a romantic proposal and the big wedding that unites both sides of the family. You hold faithful to the wedding etiquette that states 'something old, something new, something borrowed, something blue' and will be happy with traditional wedding vows.

Anyone who marries you marries into your family, as you highly value family and loved ones dear to your heart. If you're a typical Cancer, you will remain close to your family throughout your life-time. If this is true for you, your other half will have to get used to family dropping in, and family holidays and get-togethers.

It's also important that you find a partner who can cope with your unpredictable nature. Someone calm might fit the bill, or someone who doesn't take everything personally.

You often learn the most about yourself through your close relationships. Even though your deep emotions can be a blessing in love, you need to be careful that you don't use your emotions to manipulate or control your partner. The reverse is also true, in that it doesn't help to hide your true feelings, especially when you're feeling hurt.

Therefore, for both these reasons, it is important to build up your self-esteem so that you don't rely on your other half to complete you. As a Cancer you can be very impressionable, and you often experience the whole gamut of emotions, including jealousy, resentment and guilt.

Strong emotions often kick in when you're worried about losing your partner. Your tendency to cling means that you hang on dearly to the one you love, sometimes way past a relationship's sell-by date. You worry about being lonely or have fears around your security if a relationship were to break down.

As you're typically an emotional and changeable individual, it can be hard for you to be firm with yourself. You know you need to knock a relationship on the head, but then you start to get romantic and remember the good times, and you would do anything for a cuddle and affection.

You are one of the star signs who's most likely to keep mementoes of past loves or diaries that recount your romantic experiences. You find it hard to let go of your feelings and sometimes you have to tap into the side of your nature that feels upset and betrayed if you are to move on.

Ideally for you though, a love relationship will last for ever, and you'll grow old together with many happy memories to share. Be careful that you don't procrastinate in love, however, and get so used to a comfortable lifestyle that you put off creating experiences and memories together.

Your Love Matches

Some star signs are a better love match for you than others. The classic combinations are the other two star signs from the same element as your sign, water; in Cancer's case, Scorpio and Pisces.

Ideally, you want a relationship that offers you plenty of affection, with a partner who will remain faithful by your side and make you feel secure, both emotionally and financially. A relationship can be a status symbol for you or fulfil a deep need to feel protected.

It's also important to recognise that any star sign match can be a good match if you're willing to learn from each other and use astrological insight to understand more about what makes the other person tick. Here's a quick guide to your love matches with all twelve star signs:

Cancer–Aries: Squaring Up To Each Other

This can be an instant attraction triggered by intense needs, but you must realise that if desire tips over into neediness, independent Aries will be off like a shot. You bring out the little boy or girl within Aries, and the 'child' (Aries) responds to your 'motherly' (Cancer) ways.

Cancer–Taurus: Sexy Sextiles

You are natural nurturers and share a mutual love of food and comfort. This is a classic 'earth mother' combination, and healthy pursuits or a country lifestyle are all this match needs to live happily ever after. Another ideal scenario is a big family to care for and look after together.

Cancer–Gemini: Next-Door Neighbours

You need a partner who understands you on an emotional level, but Gemini runs a mile from too much emotion. If they can help transform and understand your mood swings and keep things light, while you nurture childlike Gemini, this pairing can go far.

Cancer–Cancer: Two Peas In A Pod

The two of you are great together if you focus on homemaking, feeding each other and snuggling up cosy and warm. Playing happy families is your forte. Problems arise when you both experience moody moments, as there's no place in a relationship for simultaneous sulking.

Cancer–Leo: Next-Door Neighbours

Your emotional nature thrives on the heat and warmth of fun-loving Leo. Leo loves to be the centre of attention and laps up your caring and protective side. Treats and indulgences are a necessity not a luxury in this relationship, as this is the right road to pampering heaven.

Cancer–Virgo: Sexy Sextiles

This relationship is super-caring, and you are both happy to lead a routine lifestyle. You enjoy taking care of each other but should avoid being critical. The little things in life make the biggest difference, and there'll be no shortage of cuddle sessions in this comfy combination.

Cancer–Libra: Squaring Up To Each Other

This relationship has a feminine vibe marked by kindness. Both of you ease into attachment relationships and enjoy having loved ones close by who you can rely on. As long as you share or appreciate Libra's sense of style, this is a comfortable and artistic combination.

Cancer–Scorpio: In Your Element

You two share a capacity for intimacy, plus there's a side to both of you that enjoys quiet and a place to retreat from the outside world. If you keep the waves of emotion flowing and allow the light to enter into your most hidden areas, you two can happily sail off into the sunset together.

Cancer–Sagittarius: Soulmates

Your two signs of the zodiac are poles apart. Sagittarius is the traveller of the zodiac and Cancer rules home and family. One craves security (Cancer), the other fights against it (Sagittarius). Finding the right environment that works for both is the key to happiness.

Cancer–Capricorn: Opposites Attract

You need comfort and nourishment, and you take pride in nurturing family and friends. Capricorn is the workaholic of the zodiac, who aspires to great things and is a responsible and secure partner. This can be a warm, safe connection as you provide for and protect each other.

Cancer–Aquarius: Soulmates

Emotional Cancer and logical Aquarius may seem an odd match, but this pairing can work. Aquarius loves to solve problems, and your sign of Cancer is an emotional enigma. If the relationship becomes your primary focus, there's plenty to keep this match interesting.

Cancer–Pisces: In Your Element

You two are super-sweet and want to take care of each other. There's a gentle vulnerability about this combination and kindness and caring play a big part in the relationship. The tears are turned on more than usual, so it may end up becoming too wet if the waterworks turn into a monsoon.

Your Sex Life

· · · · ·

People often think of you as being cautious and timid, which is something of a myth when it comes to sexual pleasure. In fact, your strong desire for intimacy and connection is a great motivator, and you're perfectly capable of being proactive when it comes to propositioning a potential lover.

You are, however, a compassionate soul, which is why you often sidle into physical relationships, rarely wearing your heart on your sleeve, for fear of being vulnerable or getting hurt. Sometimes you pretend that you're blasé about sex, although underneath that's rarely true.

Being one of the emotional water signs, you also have an incredible depth of feeling and sensuous passion that wants and needs to be expressed. Your natural instinct to look after and care for other people also has a role to play in your physical relationships.

You might even have a propensity to leap into bed with someone to cheer them up or because they want you to. Ensure you get your own needs met, however, rather than just having sex to make the other person happy.

In bed, you thrive on loving, intimate embraces and you are the zodiac's cuddle machine. Curling your arms and legs around your partner as you make love satisfies the caring streak within you.

For the Cancer woman, your breasts are your erogenous zone and super-sensitive, and you delight in pressing them close to your lover. A man's chest can be a huge turn-on and another area of the body that's special for your sign. The Cancer man is often turned on by breasts too, as they represent the maternal and feminine side of a woman.

Both sexes love to feel nurtured and to be intimate with another human being. Ideally, however, there must be an emotional connection before you're ready to indulge fully in the sexual act.

Sex for you can turn into a ritual, and you might enjoy bathing together before you move into the bedroom. A romantic environment awakens your inner sensuality and you enjoy sex with the lights turned off, so you can experience each other's bodies primarily through the sense of touch.

Honour and respect are an integral part of the sexual act for the typical Cancer. Once you're with an intimate partner who loves and cherishes your body, this leads to a deeper lovemaking experience that's fulfilling in all the right ways.

After lovemaking, you enjoy falling asleep snuggling up close to your lover; it's rare for you to be happy with a partner who leaves you straight after sex.

Instead, you usually prefer lazy mornings in bed or sharing breakfast after a night of passion. It's important that you feel valued for who you are once you've shared sexual intimacy with another person. Otherwise, that overly sensitive nature can kick in.

As a Cancer woman, you tend to be a mother first, a lover second, which can prove a challenge once you have kids. There's a second wave to womanhood, however, and your libido often leaps into overdrive once your children have left the nest.

CANCER ON A FIRST DATE

- you invite them to your place for a meal

- you dress for comfort

- you want your date to take the lead

- you are impressed by a caring nature

- you talk about your families

Your Friends and Family

Your sign of Cancer is one of the introvert signs of the zodiac. This doesn't mean that you want to spend all your time on your own, although if you have a cosy place to call home, sometimes it takes a lot to prise you out of your comfort zone.

Friendships are important to you, however, and you consider lasting friendships some of your greatest achievements. As the past is so significant for you, you might have good friends from schooldays, or perhaps you've chosen to settle down close to where you grew up.

Your real friends are the ones you can come back to after a long time apart, and you still slot into each other's lives with ease. It's the comfy-slippers type of friendship rather than anything spiky or awkward that appeals to your routine-loving Cancer nature.

You do sometimes let old friendships drift, often because you don't get round to being in touch. It doesn't mean you don't care, but you can get caught up in the routine of life and find it hard to break out or make an effort to reconnect.

Like anything in Cancer's life, friendships work best when they fit in comfortably to your routine, and you meet on a regular basis. It's via your friendships that you can express the soft and silly side of your nature. The word 'loony' comes from 'lunar', relating to your ruler, the Moon, and having friends who you can go crazy with can be a great release for your complex emotional nature.

You don't want to put on a big act around your friends; instead, you're happy to have friends with whom you feel completely relaxed. You will usually have one or two dear friends who you like to see on a regular basis or catch up with as often as life allows.

If you're a typical Cancer, you are an excellent mimic, and many comedians were born under your sign. One of the most famous of recent years is Peter Kay (2 July), a cuddly but often outrageous character whose comedy is based on everyday observations. He even wrote an award-winning series about a commute to work, *Car Share.* Your archetypal Cancer can find the funny side of life in the most ordinary of circumstances.

Your fickle nature does make for complicated friendships, and you can take a sudden dislike to certain friends or colleagues if you find their behaviour annoying. You might be all sweetness and light to their face but end up talking about them to other friends. You like to portray the fact that you're fun-loving and kind, but you do have the odd crabby put-down that can offend.

Sincerity is a core value in your friendships, and you're not impressed by friends who put on a big show or try to be someone they're not. Flashy parties and social climbing aren't usually your thing either, and you're happier with an intimate gathering and being around people you know well. Your ideal social get-together is meeting up with a few friends for drinks and laughs or having dinner round your place.

Family plays a huge role in your Cancer psyche, and the usual scenario is that you remain close to your immediate family. Some Cancer men will openly admit they're 'Mummy's boy' and some Cancer women are incredibly close to their mum or sisters. You often find it's the Cancer child too who connects most deeply to a grandparent; if so, the bond will remain for a lifetime.

These strong ties between you and your family can't be easily broken. Having family you love and who love you in return helps to create a feeling of security and connectedness, which fulfils the Cancer soul on a deep level.

If you choose to have your own family, this is a natural progression for you. In fact, becoming a parent can be an integral part of your vocation, and you're often a natural at motherhood or fatherhood.

Having children or animals to look after taps into your caring nature and makes you feel needed and useful. More than that, however, you have a natural gift with children, especially any who are troubled or misunderstood. You want to sweep them up into your ample bosom and protect them from the outside world.

Letting go of your children can be a double-edged sword, however, because you find it hard to do, even though you've prepared them well for their transition into adulthood. Typically, when your children leave the family nest, you'll flit back and forth doing what the Cancer mum or dad does best: feeding them, looking after them, nurturing them.

Your Health and Well-Being

KEY CONCEPTS: home cooking, daily exercise, take care of your gut, relax in water, indulgent creamy desserts

The whole idea of keeping fit can be a puzzle to the typical Cancer. When you're running around doing cooking, housework, gardening, DIY, shopping and any other number of household and daily activities, that can seem like enough to the traditional Cancer.

In fact, you tend to keep fit and healthy when you organise your day around your schedule and plan your fitness accordingly. For example, if you get off the train or bus a stop or two early and walk for twenty minutes on the way to work, that can suit you better than making time for the gym or an exercise class.

It is wise, however, to ensure that you do the necessary minimum concerning your fitness and even incorporating a walk into your daily routine will do wonders for the Cancer physique. You are one of the star signs who is prone to being over-weight, firstly because you are one of life's comfort eaters and secondly because it can take a lot to prise you out of a place of comfort.

So find what works for you. Water is Cancer's element and swimming is the obvious choice, or water aerobics, or perhaps kayaking or sailing. Water is an excellent element in which to relax, either in a long bath or by taking yourself off to a spa or steam room.

Drinking plenty of water is a must for you to be healthy too and if you're a typical Cancer, you can suffer from fluid retention. Your sign rules the breasts, chest and stomach and it's important to pay particular attention to these areas of your body.

If you're a Cancer woman, learn to love your breasts; check them regularly and indulge in massage to the breasts if it works for you. You often love belly dancing, and this can be a brilliant exercise for strengthening your torso.

If you're keen to get fit, head to the gym. Exercises that focus on upper body strength and firming your inner core can make a big difference not only to your posture but to your self-esteem and confidence as well.

Cancer's ruling planetary body, the Moon, appears in our language in the words 'month' and 'menses'. The cycle of the Moon is in sync with the menstrual cycle, and the Moon's monthly cycle can be helpful to the Cancer woman.

Ideally, you want to be in flow, which is necessary for your fertility, and this is often connected to how well-balanced you feel emotionally. The mooncup, a natural way of catching your monthly flow of blood, is perfect for your sign.

Your retentive nature means that you can tend not to express yourself fully, which can have a knock-on effect on your stomach and gut. Both Cancer women and men need to learn to let their emotions flow and trust their gut. Holding on to feelings can have a detrimental effect on your well-being. Yours is a sign that can suffer from food allergies or eating disorders when you're growing up.

Learning to love yourself and care for yourself isn't a given for the typical Cancer. You do so much for other people that it's easy to leave your-self out. It's worth remembering, however, that you can only care for others well if you care for yourself first. Prioritise self-care and ensure that looking after your well-being becomes a natural daily habit.

Cancer and Food

The classic Cancer is a natural cook, and you make an excellent chef. You not only have an innate understanding of good food but you enjoy feeding and nourishing the ones you love too.

Home cooking is Cancer's domain, and you often have recipes that have been passed down through the generations. Your love of cooking can be a nod to traditions, in keeping with the Cancer archetype. Many Cancer individuals will have learned about enjoyment of food and cooking via their mothers, fathers or grandparents.

Your sign rules the stomach and this part of your body can be particularly susceptible to stress. Therefore, it is important that you allow yourself time to digest food properly and don't rush meals. Sitting down for a family meal is an ideal Cancer pastime because it not only brings everyone together but also means you can savour your food and take your time eating.

You are often an emotional eater, and you tend to put on weight when you're going through a difficult period in your life. In fact, it's quite hard for your sign of Cancer to keep the weight off, and your love of food often means that you would anyway rather be curvaceous and radiant than skinny and unhappy.

All planetary bodies rule certain foods and your ruler, the Moon, is linked to foods that contain water and are cool and moist. These include such foods as celery, lettuce, cucumber and melon and can be extended to sushi and raw food generally. Seafood such as lobster, crab or shrimp is also a Cancer delicacy.

It's not all healthy fare that sings to the Cancer individual. The Moon rules dairy foods, milk, cheese and yoghurt. If you do find yourself wanting to lose weight, it's wise to start by removing desserts from your Cancer menu. It's imperative for your Cancer soul, though, that you remain a lover of food rather than get to a place in your life where food is the enemy.

Do You Look Like A Cancer?

The element of water flows, and there is often a gracefulness and a slow ease in the way you walk. If something's urgent, however, you won't hesitate to rush, taking short steps rather than long. Some Cancer individuals scuttle like their zodiac symbol, the Crab, especially the non-confrontational, shy Cancer type.

Cancer women, in particular, are blessed with curvaceous figures, and there's a voluptuousness or stockiness to the typical physique. Cancer rules the breasts, chest and stomach and the Cancer figure is primarily round or soft.

The Cancer face is often beautiful like the Moon and tends to be round-shaped with a broad fore-head and luminous, sometimes pale skin. The lips are usually round and distinctive.

Like all of the water signs, people notice a Cancer person's eyes first, and your sign has a wide-eyed look. Sometimes the eyes show sadness, and you can always see the emotion in them.

Your Style and Image

Your ruler, the Moon, is one of two female planetary bodies in astrology, the other being Venus.
The Moon is Madame to Venus' Mademoiselle,
and the Moon symbolises the beauty of the full-
ness of woman, all curves and lusciousness.

Cancer isn't defined by the skinny catwalk model
but rather the superbly feminine hourglass figure,
the generous belly, the magnificent cleavage. If
you have a typically curvaceous Cancer figure,

flaunt it. Wear wrap dresses, outfits that cinch the waist, soft materials that cling and low cut tops and show off the best parts of your body.

Cancer men look good when they bulk up and can show off their impressive pecs with a figure-hugging top. Soft jumpers in cashmere and wool highlight Cancer's loveable nature, as do shirts in soft cotton, preferably not tucked in!

Flowing clothes and layers work well for both sexes, and pay particular attention to your neckline. Being a Sun Cancer you don't have a distinct look, although jeans and a white T-shirt are ideal go-to garments for everyday wear.

Indeed, you often wear different clothes to suit your changing moods. Traditionally, subtle colours work well for Cancer, such as white, pale blue and light grey, but usually you have outfits in a myriad of colours, to wear depending on whether you feel happy and confident, or melancholy and deep. You have a natural sense of style, and an artistic flair for colour, cut and image that means coordinating your outfits is a breeze.

The Cancer wardrobe is rarely minimalist, but instead, you might have garments that you've held on to for years. Vintage clothes are often your thing, or clothes that have been handed down to you, especially if your mother/father was a style icon back in the day. You don't spend a fortune on clothes either because you have a great eye for a bargain and enjoy the sales.

A typical Cancer appreciates antique jewellery or sentimental items – a locket with a photo of your family or you as a child. Pearl and shell are ideal accessories for your sign and silver jewellery and watches suit you too.

Plenty of comfy clothes are a must for the home, whether PJs or loose sports gear that you can lounge around in.

Your Home

Your Ideal Cancer Home:

Your ideal home is a retreat, a place where you can rest and unwind from the stresses of the outside world. When you own your family home, and it's just as you like it, you wouldn't want to be anywhere else.

Cancer is the star sign most closely associated with the home. Think of your zodiac symbol, the

73

Crab, who carries his outer shell around with him, and you get an idea of how important home, safety and privacy are for your sign.

If you're a typical Cancer, you have a changeable nature and your moods ebb and flow, in tune with your ruler, the Moon. This is why it's important that you have a restful space, somewhere you can withdraw from life outside and curl up in comfort.

The relaxed ambience of your home is geared towards harmony, a place where your loved ones feel nurtured and you can indulge the romantic side of your nature. You're not usually into grandiose gestures, and you don't need your home to be a showcase to impress others.

Instead, your home must feel lived in, with solid pieces of furniture, both reliable and durable, as well as plenty of soft, rounded features – ample throws and cushions, rugs and covers that you can lounge on to your heart's content. Preferably in front of an open fire or another feature that's symbolic of warmth and cosiness.

The colours associated with your sign of Cancer are all colours linked to the moon – white, silver, mother-of-pearl and any shimmery or translucent colours. In particular, white, the colour of purity and simplicity, appeals to the gentle side of your nature. You may choose delicate, sheer curtains in soft fabrics that filter the harsh light of day.

You love flowers in your home, big vases of white roses, lilies or a simple bunch of tulips. Objects hold fond memories for you too, and you have personal belongings and possessions scattered all over the place.

You adore coloured glass and silver, especially photo frames, which take pride of place when they contain pictures of your family and loved ones. You like to be surrounded by beautiful things, and you often have an appreciation for literature, music and art.

Being a romantic soul, you hold on to things, which is why you have a reputation for being a hoarder. Similarly, once you've found a piece of furniture you like, you'll keep it until it's old and shabby. You can get so attached to your possessions that an old leather chair or pine dresser feels like an old friend.

Your taste can be old-fashioned as you're a traditionalist and you are often attracted to antique furniture or jewellery, especially if there's a story behind it. Whether it's an old grandfather clock passed down through the generations or a charity shop find that reminds you of your childhood, you love the sense of continuity that memories offer.

The kitchen is often a warm and vibrant room in your home, and you love nothing more than having your favourite people around a large table, where you can feed and nourish them.

After the kitchen, the bathroom tends to be your favourite room in the home, and it will often be a luxurious hideaway. You love relaxing bath oils, big white fluffy towels and candlelight – your private sanctuary where you can soak in comfort.

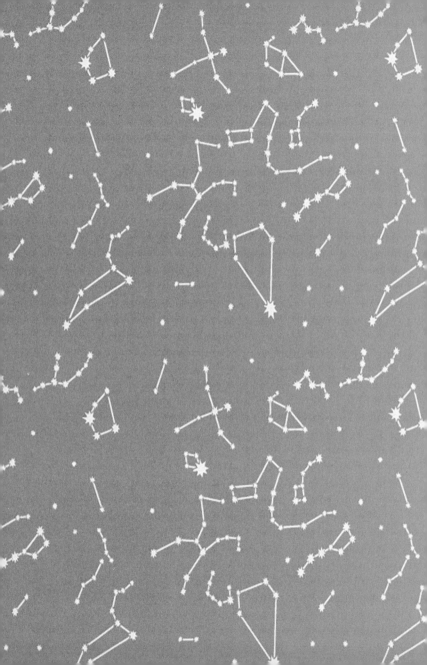

Your Star Sign Destinations

IDEAS FOR CANCER:

- *go on a trip to discover your ancestry*

- *an all-inclusive family holiday at a five-star resort*

- *a cosy log cabin by a lake with your folks*

Did you know that many cities and countries are ruled by a particular star sign? This is based on

when a country was founded, although sometimes, depending on their history, places have
more than one star sign attributed to them.

This can help you decide where to travel to and
it can also explain why there are certain places
where you feel at home straight away.

When it comes to holidays and trips around the
world, first of all you have to winkle yourself out
of your shell. If anyone is going to be a homebody
and love spending time at home, it's you. When
it comes to your two weeks' summer holiday, you
might choose to spend it redecorating at home
or spend your time doing nothing and nesting.

Family holidays were made for you, and you often
prefer to get all the family together for a big
holiday or go and see relatives who live in
far-flung destinations. You would have no qualms
about flying to the other side of the earth if it
meant catching up with loved ones. Indeed, if you
have family who you love, it's hard for you to

stay away when you have free time, wherever they are located.

Travelling in your own country can also be a dream holiday for you as there is a side of your nature that's cautious and a creature of habit. You don't always find it easy to step out of your comfort zone, which is why you can sometimes talk yourself out of more adventurous trips away.

Being by water is soothing for your soul and a canal holiday would be perfect for you, steering your home calmly down the waterways. Anywhere you can unwind, preferably without lots of people and noise, is the ideal Cancer break. A boating holiday would be perfect too if you have your sea legs.

You are often drawn back towards the past, and you have a love of all things historical. If you can take in some local culture, old churches and interesting art galleries, that ticks a lot of boxes for the perfect Cancer holiday. You could choose to go abroad or opt instead for a delightful town close to your home.

Countries ruled by Cancer include Holland, Scotland, the USA, New Zealand, Algeria, Paraguay, Tunisia

Cities ruled by Cancer include Manchester in the UK; Amsterdam in Holland; Istanbul in Turkey; Venice and Milan in Italy; New York in the USA; Tokyo in Japan; Cadiz in Spain; Stockholm in Sweden

Your Career and Vocation

KEY CONCEPTS: regular employment, a caring career, home and family professions, emotional intelligence

Security is an important motivation for the classic Cancer, and you are happiest in a job that offers steadiness. Until or unless you recognise your leadership qualities, you are more likely to settle for a safe prospect career-wise and a job that promises longevity and stability over contract work or an unpredictable lifestyle.

You like to feel comfortable in your work environment, and you always create a home-from-home feel in your office or work surroundings; a corner where you feel cosy and can slip easily into regular habits. The ability to make a nice cup of tea and have time for a lunch break can be a big deal for the routine-loving Cancer.

The people you work with are important too, because when you feel 'part of the family' you're more motivated to work hard. You're unlikely to excel in a cut-throat industry or a tough or competitive environment, although there are exceptions to the rule.

On the whole, however, you thrive best when you work alongside people with whom you share an emotional connection, and you work together happily as a team. A company that excels in training and customer service, and cares about its employees and their work–life balance, ticks a lot of boxes for the Cancer employee.

Caring is a principal Cancer concept and when it comes to the right career, you are at your best in a role where you can look after other people. In particular, you often end up looking after the people at opposite ends of the life spectrum: the young – children and babies – or the elderly.

You have a deep respect for the so-called 'weaker' members of society, and you're more likely to see their inherent value than anyone else. Feeling needed makes you feel appreciated in return, and to you this is preferable to working in a cold or impersonal environment where people are disregarded in favour of numbers and product success. You soon lose your way if a job has no deeper meaning than raking in the money or bringing in the business.

Your high level of emotional intelligence can be a valuable tool in many professions. The classic Cancer flies high in life when you find a way to express your emotions artistically or creatively through whatever you do.

Don't underestimate the power of your emotions to make a difference in the world. You connect with other people through your emotions, and once you've established a relationship, then you can begin to encourage and inspire others once they feel seen, noticed and heard.

Your particular leadership style tends to be caring and nurturing, and it's often your love for other people and your desire to make life more comfortable and safe for others that spurs you on. You know how important it is to feel safe and secure, and you want to ensure that other people can enjoy the basic needs of life.

Many Cancer leaders rise to the top of their profession because they take care of their employees or they bring the personal element into their professional role. For example, Richard Branson (18 July) is renowned for thinking of his Virgin business enterprise as 'one big family', and he has often invited star Virgin employees to spend time with his own family.

Angela Merkel (17 July), the Chancellor of Germany, is known by the German people as 'Mutti', the German for 'Mother'. One of the most iconic Cancer individuals is Nelson Mandela (18 July), who is often thought of as the father of South Africa. In fact, many people call him 'Tata', a Xhosa word for 'Father'. Cancer's love of family often extends to nations and the entire human race.

The two areas of family and home are often popular career choices for you. A family business, uniting family, organising family events, for example. A job in real estate or interior design, working with refugees or the homeless or creating more sustainable homes.

In the future, the Moon, your astrological ruler, might even become a place to call home. Two businessmen involved in big plans to find a new home in outer space are both Sun Cancer individuals: Elon Musk, founder of SpaceX, and Richard Branson, founder of Virgin Galactic.

The past, too, is a place where you can allow your imagination to run wild. You have a natural affinity for history and archiving, for remembering the past, and this is where your sentimental nature can play a valuable role.

If you're seeking inspiration for a new job, take a look at the list below, which reveals the traditional careers that come under the Cancer archetype:

TRADITIONAL CANCER CAREERS

chef
estate agent
interior designer
schoolteacher

nursery teacher

antique dealer

historian

homemaker

foster-parent

midwife

publican

B&B owner

au pair/nanny

lifeguard

wine taster

cleaner

care worker

museum curator

store manager

customer service representative

Your Money and Prosperity

You can often be successful when it comes to money matters because of your need for security. You are not typically one of life's gamblers; instead, you want to ensure you have, at the bare minimum, a roof over your head and regular employment.

If you're typical of your sign of Cancer, you'll be the individual who starts a savings account as a child and keeps on saving throughout adulthood. You take a sensible approach to finances on the whole and plan for the future.

In fact, you can be one of the most frugal of all the star signs, if needs be, and be happy making do with what you have and saving for the future, rather than going wild and blowing your money on a whim.

Home ownership is a natural progression for the Cancer individual and this ticks a lot of boxes in your journey towards fulfilment and happiness. In fact, owning your home can be the ultimate Cancer goal. If you can grab the opportunity to buy and sell properties to make money and make progress financially, even better.

You're not one of life's natural risk-takers, however, and you are more likely to be drawn towards the tried and tested approach to prosperity than taking a huge leap into the unknown. Home and family are your safe-fail routes towards wealth, whether in the shape of inheritance, family heirlooms or moving into the family home.

There is, however, a drawback in the Cancer approach to money. You can be so loath to risk or spend when it comes to money that you end up downsizing your life to an extreme degree, becoming stuck in a place of scarcity and losing your ability to enjoy life's abundance and benefit from the flow of money.

You have to consider this carefully and weigh up all the options; otherwise you could lose out by holding on tight and clinging to what's yours. You might choose to keep hold of your money in case of the proverbial rainy day, but in the process, you can lose out on living in the present.

You are one of life's hoarders and there comes a time in every hoarder's life when they need to check whether the time is right to sell. Don't hold on to things in your life for so long that they end up having no value at all.

As a Cancer individual, it is sometimes necessary that you learn to release the past so you can live fully in the present day. Don't deny yourself life's riches and the full abundance that's available to you right here, right now.

Your Cosmic Gifts and Talents

Moon Child

You are the only sign of the zodiac to be ruled by the Moon, and your emotions are often in flux during its phases. Notice whether you turn into a 'lunatic', which derives from the word 'luna' – moon – during the full moon, and become overly emotional. If so, try not to start a big argument at this point.

You can take Moon knowledge further and learn the best times in the month to diet, to have your hair cut or to plant and harvest food for optimum success. There's a whole system of lunar gardening called biodynamics. Use this to your advantage and get in sync with the Moon's cycle.

Family Values

Family values are often passed down over generations. They help to bring structure into your life, through daily habits such as eating together with family or sharing housework. They also represent a moral code by which to live, including behaviours that are honest, sincere, kind and helpful to other people and the community.

Cancer's role is deeply rooted within the family, and you too can be the bearer of solid family values, whether you experienced a model childhood or not. It's perhaps even more important to establish strong family values in your own life if you weren't lucky enough to experience them as a child.

Home Comforts

You are a genius at creating a comfortable home for yourself and the people you love, even if your surroundings aren't grand. You have a natural ability to make the place you live a cosy retreat, somewhere you can cook for other people, feed the ones you love, stock up on lovely food and bring warmth and kindness into other people's lives. Allow your protective nature to have full rein in the place you live and create a refuge for yourself and others.

Document The Past

Cancer is the sign most closely linked to the past, thanks to Cancer's natural rulership of the fourth house, at the base of the horoscope. Honour your past connections by drawing up your family tree, collecting recipes or stories from your childhood, hoarding old family photos or conversing with your elders. We lose sight of our history if it's not documented, valued and respected, and you play a vital role in breathing life into the past.

Celebrate Your Curves

Cancer is the epitome of woman and soft, feminine qualities. Whatever your sex, shape or size, learn to love your body and the softness of your skin and revel in Cancer's deliciousness. If you're curvy or cuddly, flaunt it, and remind the world of the beauty of the natural body.

The gorgeous Gisele Bündchen (20 July) stormed onto catwalks in the late 90s and was hailed as 'The Body' and seen as a welcome change from the rail-thin models with the 'heroin chic' look that had previously dominated the modelling world.

Find Someone To Mother

In astrology your ruler, the Moon, is the traditional symbol of the mother. So find someone or something to 'mother' in life, to look after, to care for, to protect and nurture. This might be your children, an elderly relative, your pets or your beloved house plants.

You might choose to adopt a child or pet, become a foster-parent, care for a friend's child or volunteer for a charity. This is part of your vocation in life, so use your skills of mothering and caring to the full.

One of the world's most famous mothers was Princess Diana (1 July), who married into the British royal family but was renowned for her love of her two boys and her wish for them to lead as normal a life as possible. Her son, Prince William (21 June), heir to the throne, is also a Sun Cancer, and no doubt his mother's legacy will live on through him and his children.

Emotional Artist

Water signs like yourself respond to the world emotionally and it is important that you find an outlet for this passionate side of your nature. The worlds of music, art and film often resonate with you, and there's an artistic, imaginative soul in the quintessential Cancer.

When you access this part of the Cancer psyche, it can enrich and deepen your experience of life and positively impact other people's lives. Tracey Emin (3 July) chose a classic Cancer symbol of comfort in her famous art installation, *My Bed*.

Films, Books, Music

• • • • •

Films: *In The Mood For Love*, director, Wong Kar-Wai (17 July) and starring Tony Leung (27 June) or *Il Postino*, a film about Pablo Neruda (12 July)

Books: *The Da Vinci Code* by Dan Brown (22 June) or *Wolf Hall* by Hilary Mantel (6 July)

Music: 'The Boys Of Summer' by Don Henley (22 July) or any number of songs about the magical Moon – 'Man On The Moon' by R.E.M., 'The Whole Of The Moon' by The Waterboys, 'Fly Me To The Moon' by Frank Sinatra or 'Moondance' by Van Morrison

YOGA POSE:

Happy Baby: stretches and soothes the inner
groin and lower back

TAROT CARD:

The Moon!

GIFTS TO BUY A CANCER:

- waterproof mascara, for the emotional Cancer
- fluffy cushions or a cosy throw
- a voucher for a celebrity cooking class
- a keepsake box
- a set of Booker Prize-winning novels
- a romantic classical music CD
- heirloom china or silver cutlery
- a hot tub
- family photo session
- Star Gift – pay off their mortgage

Cancer Celebrities Born On Your Birthday

JUNE

 (Prince William – born on the cusp, see Q&A)

 Billy Wilder, Prunella Scales, Dan Brown, Esther Rantzen, Meryl Streep, Carson Daly, Cyndi Lauper, Emmanuelle Seigner

23 Alan Turing, Bob Fosse, Randy Jackson, Frances McDormand, June Carter Cash, Zinedine Zidane, Selma Blair, Duffy, Jason Mraz, Stuart Sutcliffe, Bip Ling

 24 Michele Lee, Adrienne Shelly, Lionel Messi, Ned Rocknroll, Solange Knowles

 25 Carly Simon, Ricky Gervais, George Michael, Anthony Bourdain, Sheridan Smith

 26 Georgie Fame, Chris O'Donnell, Gretchen Wilson, Ariana Grande, King Bach, Aubrey Plaza

 27 Helen Keller, Vera Wang, Tony Leung, Isabelle Adjani, Tobey Maguire, Matthew Lewis, Sam Claflin, Khloe Kardashian

 28 Gilda Radner, Richard Rodgers, Mel Brooks, Clarissa Dickson Wright, Kathy Bates, John Cusack, Elon Musk

29 Gary Busey, Nicole Scherzinger, Katherine
Jenkins

 30 Mike Tyson, Lena Horne, Michael
Phelps, James Martin, Cheryl Cole, Tom
Burke

JULY

 1 Carl Lewis, Debbie Harry, Dan Aykroyd,
Princess Diana, Ross Kemp, David
Prowse, Pamela Anderson, Missy Elliott,
Claire Forlani, Liv Tyler, Léa Seydoux

 2 Jerry Hall, Peter Kay, Ashley Tisdale,
Lindsay Lohan, Margot Robbie

 3 Tom Stoppard, Ken Russell, Tom Cruise,
Tracey Emin, Sandra Lee, Julian Assange,
Julie Burchill

 4 Neil Simon, Gina Lollobrigida, Neil
Morrissey, Ronni Ancona

5 Paul Smith, Huey Lewis, Amélie Mauresmo, Eva Green

6 Janet Leigh, Frida Kahlo, Bill Haley, Nancy Reagan, Dalai Lama, George Bush, Hilary Mantel, Sylvester Stallone, Richard Beckinsale, Geoffrey Rush, Jennifer Saunders, 50 Cent, Kevin Hart

7 Ringo Starr, Bill Oddie, Jeremy Kyle, Shelley Duvall, Michelle Kwan, Jack Whitehall

8 John D. Rockefeller, Monty Don, Anjelica Huston, Pauline Quirke, Robert Knepper, Toby Keith, Kevin Bacon, Beck, Ellen MacArthur, Milo Ventimiglia, Jaden Smith, Sophia Bush

9 Barbara Cartland, Richard Wilson, O. J. Simpson, David Hockney, Tom Hanks, Courtney Love, Jack White

Arthur Ashe, Ronnie James Dio, John Simm, Chiwetel Ejiofor, Jessica Simpson, Perrie Edwards, Sofía Vergara, Adam Hills

 Giorgio Armani, Craig Charles, Greg Grunberg, Justin Chambers, Lil' Kim, Nadya Suleman

 Pablo Neruda, Bill Cosby, Gaby Roslin, Anna Friel, Michelle Rodriguez, Topher Grace, Malala Yousafzai

 Cheech Marin, Patrick Stewart, Harrison Ford, Ian Hislop, Lisa Riley, Samia Ghadie, Tulisa, Sharon Horgan

 Gertrude Bell, Gerald Ford, Gustav Klimt, Woody Guthrie, Ingmar Bergman, Jane Lynch, Matthew Fox, David Mitchell, Lee Mead, Phoebe Waller-Bridge, Maxine Peake

15 Terry O'Quinn, Jesse Ventura, Linda Ronstadt, Forest Whitaker, Brigitte Nielsen, Beth Ostrosky, Brian Austin Green, Jill Halfpenny, Diane Kruger, Ian Curtis

 16 Ginger Rogers, Barbara Stanwyck, Michael Flatley, Will Ferrell, Corey Feldman, Jayma Mays

17 Phyllis Diller, Donald Sutherland, James Cagney, Camilla Parker Bowles, Angela Merkel, Wong Kar-Wai, Wayne Sleep, David Hasselhoff, Fern Britton, Gino D'Acampo, Darren Day, Konnie Huq, Tom Fletcher, Carey Hart, Luke Bryan

 18 Red Skelton, Nelson Mandela, Hunter S. Thompson, Richard Branson, Wendy Williams, Vin Diesel, Kristen Bell, Elizabeth Gilbert, Priyanka Chopra, M.I.A.

19 Nicola Sturgeon, Jared Padalecki, Brian May, Benedict Cumberbatch

 20 Diana Rigg, Carlos Santana, Natalie Wood, Wendy Richard, Terri Irwin, Julian Rhind-Tutt, Rhys Ifans, Josh Holloway, Chris Cornell, Gisele Bündchen, Anton du Beke, Tim Ferriss

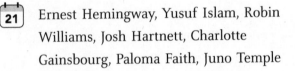 **21** Ernest Hemingway, Yusuf Islam, Robin Williams, Josh Hartnett, Charlotte Gainsbourg, Paloma Faith, Juno Temple

 22 Terence Stamp, Albert Brooks, Edward Hopper, Danny Glover, Don Henley, Willem Dafoe, David Spade, Stephen Mangan, Selena Gomez, Prince George

 23 (David Essex, Philip Seymour Hoffman – born on a cusp, see Q&A)

Q&A Section

• • • • •

Q. What is the difference between a Sun sign and a Star sign?

A. They are the same thing. The Sun spends one month in each of the twelve star signs every year, so if you were born on 1 January, you are a Sun Capricorn. In astronomy, the Sun is termed a star rather than a planet, which is why the two names are interchangeable. The term 'zodiac sign', too, means the same as Sun sign and Star sign and is another way of describing which one of the twelve star signs you are, e.g. Sun Capricorn.

Q. What does it mean if I'm born on the cusp?

A. Being born on the cusp means that you were born on a day when the Sun moves from one of the twelve zodiac signs into the next. However, the Sun doesn't change signs at the same time each year. Sometimes it can be a day earlier or a day later. In the celebrity birthday section of the book, names in brackets mean that this person's birthday falls into this category.

If you know your complete birth data, including the date, time and place you were born, you can find out definitively what Sun sign you are. You do this by either checking an ephemeris (a planetary table) or asking an astrologer. For example, if a baby were born on 20 January 2018, it would be Sun Capricorn if born before 03:09 GMT or Sun Aquarius if born after 03:09 GMT. A year earlier, the Sun left Capricorn a day earlier and entered Aquarius on 19 January 2017, at 21:24 GMT. Each year the time changes are slightly different.

Q. Has my sign of the zodiac changed since I was born?

A. Every now and again, the media talks about a new sign of the zodiac called Ophiuchus and about there now being thirteen signs. This means that you're unlikely to be the same Sun sign as you always thought you were.

This method is based on fixing the Sun's movement to the star constellations in the sky, and is called 'sidereal' astrology. It's used traditionally in India and other Asian countries.

The star constellations are merely namesakes for the twelve zodiac signs. In western astrology, the zodiac is divided into twelve equal parts that are in sync with the seasons. This method is called 'tropical' astrology. The star constellations and the zodiac signs aren't the same.

Astrology is based on a beautiful pattern of symmetry (see Additional Information) and it wouldn't be the same if a thirteenth sign were introduced into the pattern. So never fear, no one is going to have to say their star sign is Ophiuchus, a name nobody even knows how to pronounce!

Q. Is astrology still relevant to me if I was born in the southern hemisphere?

A. Yes, astrology is unquestionably relevant to you. Astrology's origins, however, were founded in the northern hemisphere, which is why the Spring Equinox coincides with the Sun's move into Aries, the first sign of the zodiac. In the southern hemisphere, the seasons are reversed. Babylonian, Egyptian and Greek and Roman astrology are the forebears of modern-day astrology, and all of these civilisations were located in the northern hemisphere.

• • • • •

Q. Should I read my Sun sign, Moon sign and Ascendant sign?

A. If you know your horoscope or you have drawn up an astrology wheel for the time of your birth, you will be aware that you are more than your Sun sign. The Sun is the most important star in the sky, however, because the other planets revolve around it, and your horoscope in the media is based on Sun signs. The Sun represents your essence, who you are striving to become throughout your lifetime.

The Sun, Moon and Ascendant together give you a broader impression of yourself as all three reveal further elements about your personality. If you know your Moon and Ascendant signs, you can read all three books to gain further insight into who you are. It's also a good idea to read the Sun sign book that relates to your partner, parents, children, best friends, even your boss for a better understanding of their characters too.

Q. Is astrology a mix of fate and free will?

A. Yes. Astrology is not causal, i.e. the planets don't cause things to happen in your life; instead, the two are interconnected, hence the saying 'As above, so below'. The symbolism of the planets' movements mirrors what's happening on earth and in your personal experience of life.

You can choose to sit back and let your life unfold, or you can decide the best course of action available to you. In this way, you are combining your fate and free will, and this is one of astrology's major purposes in life. A knowledge of astrology can help you live more authentically, and it offers you a fresh perspective on how best to make progress in your life.

Q. What does it mean if I don't identify with my Sun sign? Is there a reason for this?

A. The majority of people identify with their Sun sign, and it is thought that one route to fulfilment is to grow into your Sun sign. You do get the odd exception, however.

For example, a Pisces man was adamant that he wasn't at all romantic, mystical, creative or caring, all typical Pisces archetypes. It turned out he'd spent the whole of his adult life working in the oil industry and lived primarily on the sea. Neptune is one of Pisces' ruling planets and god of the sea and Pisces rules all liquids, including oil. There's the Pisces connection.

Q. What's the difference between astrology and astronomy?

A. Astrology means 'language of the stars', whereas astronomy means 'mapping of the stars'. Traditionally, they were considered one discipline, one form of study and they coexisted together for many hundreds of years. Since the dawn of the Scientific Age, however, they have split apart.

Astronomy is the scientific strand, calculating and logging the movement of the planets, whereas astrology is the interpretation of the movement of the stars. Astrology works on a symbolic and intuitive level to offer guidance and insight. It reunites you with a universal truth, a knowingness that can sometimes get lost in place of an objective, scientific truth. Both are of value.

Q. What is a cosmic marriage in astrology?

A. One of the classic indicators of a relation-ship that's a match made in heaven is the union of the Sun and Moon. When they fall close to each other in the same sign in the birth charts of you and your partner, this is called a cosmic marriage. In astrology, the Sun and Moon are the king and queen of the heavens; the Sun is a masculine energy, and the Moon a feminine energy. They represent the eternal cycle of day and night, yin and yang.

Q. What does the Saturn Return mean?

A. In traditional astrology, Saturn was the furthest planet from the Sun, representing boundaries and the end of the universe. Saturn is linked to karma and time, and represents authority, structure and responsibility. It takes Saturn twenty-nine to thirty years to make a complete cycle of the zodiac and return to the place where it was when you were born.

This is what people mean when they talk about their Saturn Return; it's the astrological coming of age. Turning thirty can be a soul-searching time, when you examine how far you've come in life and whether you're on the right track. It's a watershed moment, a reality check and a defining stage of adulthood. The decisions you make during your Saturn Return are crucial, whether they represent endings or new commitments. Either way, it's the start of an important stage in your life path.

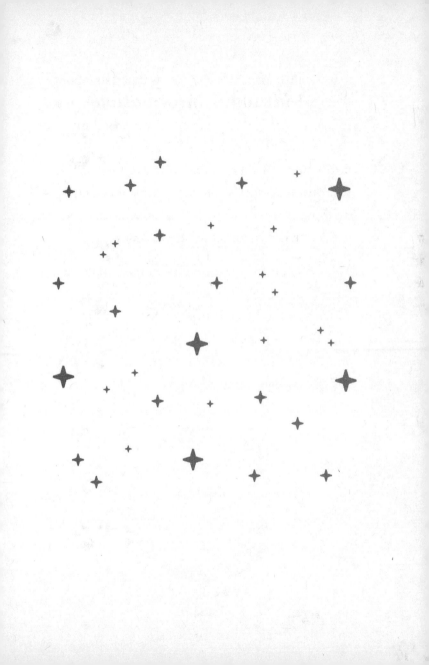

Additional Information

• • • • •

The Symmetry of Astrology

There is a beautiful symmetry to the zodiac (see horoscope wheel). There are twelve zodiac signs, which can be divided into two sets of 'introvert' and 'extrovert' signs, four elements (fire, earth, air, water), three modes (cardinal, fixed, mutable) and six pairs of opposite signs.

One of the values of astrology is in bringing opposites together, showing how they complement each other and work together and, in so doing, restore unity. The horoscope wheel represents the cyclical nature of life.

Aries *(March 21–April 19)*
Taurus *(April 20–May 20)*
Gemini *(May 21–June 20)*
Cancer *(June 21–July 22)*
Leo *(July 23–August 22)*
Virgo *(August 23–September 22)*
Libra *(September 23–October 23)*
Scorpio *(October 24–November 22)*
Sagittarius *(November 23–December 21)*
Capricorn *(December 22–January 20)*
Aquarius *(January 21–February 18)*
Pisces *(February 19–March 20)*

ELEMENTS

There are four elements in astrology and three signs allocated to each. The elements are:

fire – Aries, Leo, Sagittarius
earth – Taurus, Virgo, Capricorn
air – Gemini, Libra, Aquarius
water – Cancer, Scorpio, Pisces

What each element represents:

Fire – fire blazes bright and fire types are inspirational, motivational, adventurous and love creativity and play

Earth – earth is grounding and solid, and earth rules money, security, practicality, the physical body and slow living

Air – air is intangible and vast and air rules thinking, ideas, social interaction, debate and questioning

Water – water is deep and healing and water rules feelings, intuition, quietness, relating, giving and sharing

MODES

There are three modes in astrology and four star signs allocated to each. The modes are:

cardinal – Aries, Cancer, Libra, Capricorn
fixed – Taurus, Leo, Scorpio, Aquarius
mutable – Gemini, Virgo, Sagittarius, Pisces

What each mode represents:

Cardinal – The first group represents the leaders of the zodiac, and these signs love to initiate and take action. Some say they're controlling.

Fixed – The middle group holds fast and stands the middle ground and acts as a stable, reliable companion. Some say they're stubborn.

Mutable – The last group is more willing to go with the flow and let life drift. They're more flexible and adaptable and often dual-natured. Some say they're all over the place.

INTROVERT AND EXTROVERT SIGNS / OPPOSITE SIGNS

The introvert signs are the earth and water signs and the extrovert signs are the fire and air signs. Both sets oppose each other across the zodiac.

The 'introvert' earth and water oppositions are:

- Taurus – • Scorpio
- Cancer – • Capricorn
- Virgo – • Pisces

The 'extrovert' air and fire oppositions are:

- Aries – • Libra
- Gemini – • Sagittarius
- Leo – • Aquarius

THE HOUSES

The houses of the astrology wheel are an additional component to Sun sign horoscopes. The symmetry that is inherent within astrology remains, as the wheel is divided into twelve equal sections, called 'houses'. Each of the twelve houses is governed by one of the twelve zodiac signs.

There is an overlap in meaning as you move round the houses. Once you know the symbolism of all the star signs, it can be fleshed out further by learning about the areas of life represented by the twelve houses.

The houses provide more specific information if you choose to have a detailed birth chart reading.

This is based not only on your day of birth, which reveals your star sign, but also your time and place of birth. Here's the complete list of the meanings of the twelve houses and the zodiac sign they are ruled by:

1 – **Aries:** self, physical body, personal goals

2 – **Taurus:** money, possessions, values

3 – **Gemini:** communication, education, siblings, local neighbourhood

4 – **Cancer:** home, family, roots, the past, ancestry

5 – **Leo:** creativity, romance, entertainment, children, luck

6 – **Virgo:** work, routine, health, service

7 – **Libra:** relationships, the 'other', enemies, contracts

8 – **Scorpio:** joint finances, other people's resources, all things hidden and taboo

9 – **Sagittarius:** travel, study, philosophy, legal affairs, publishing, religion

10 – **Capricorn:** career, vocation, status, reputation

11 – **Aquarius:** friends, groups, networks, social responsibilities

12 – **Pisces:** retreat, sacrifice, spirituality

A GUIDE TO LOVE MATCHES

The star signs relate to each other in different ways depending on their essential nature. It can also be helpful to know the pattern they create across the zodiac. Here's a quick guide that relates to the chapter on Love Matches:

Two Peas In A Pod – the same star sign

Opposites Attract – star signs opposite each other

Soulmates – five or seven signs apart, and a traditional 'soulmate' connection

In Your Element – four signs apart, which means you share the same element

Squaring Up To Each Other – three signs apart, which means you share the same mode

Sexy Sextiles – two signs apart, which means you're both 'introverts' or 'extroverts'

Next Door Neighbours – one sign apart, different in nature but often share close connections